In loving memory of my brother,
Roger,
who continues to inspire me.

Designed by Claudia Schwalm in collaboration with Denise Chirpich.

Published by Cultural Connections
PO Box 1582 Alameda, CA 94501
(510) 538-8237

Printed in Hong Kong by Interprint

ISBN: 1-57371-012-1
Library of Congress Catalog Card Number: 98-094803

Cultural Connections
Home for resources in 30+ languages
URL:pwp.value.net/culture/index.htm

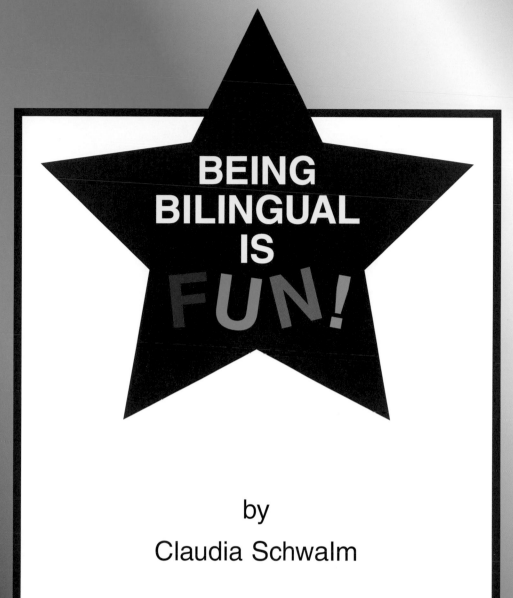

BEING BILINGUAL IS FUN!

by

Claudia Schwalm

Cultural Connections Publishing
Alameda, California

Every day all around the world, we can see and hear many different languages.

We can see signs in many languages.

Lost and Found
Objets trouvés

停車場收費處
Parking Cashier

WELCOME

ese languages are spoken in our st

いらっしゃいませ
歡迎光臨
어서 오십시오.
WELCOME
BIENVENUE
WILLKOMMEN
BUON GIORNO, PREGO
BIEN VENIDOS
MABUHAY

LIBRARY
បណ្ណាល័យ   THƯ VIỆN
BIBLIOTECA

Blé
Filamenté
24 biscuits

Délice à 100% de blé entier   500 g

EL MEXICAN
BRAND

CARAVELLE

NẤM RƠM CHÉ

We can see food labels printed in many languages.

HAPINA

GYANYAINK MESESKÖNYVE · GRANNY'S STORYBOOKS

Az ezüstkirály sípja
e Silver King's Flute

ipmesék ⊕ Hungarian Folktales

ILIPINO
SA PREP

un

MAÑOS
Francisca Altamirano

trillas

nina

We can see
books printed in
many languages.

We can see money printed in many languages.

RUSSIAN
SPANISH
SWAHILI
TAGALOG
VIETNAMESE

coat

ЛАМПА
lamp

umbrella

trai banh

ball

CULTURAL CONNECTIONS
Publishing Division of Claudia's Caravan
ALAMEDA, CALIFORNIA
(510) 814-0228

СЛОВ

Словарь. Компакт-ка

СМОТРИ
СЛУШАЙ·ЧИТАЙ
ПИШИ·ГОВОРИ

*Дружат
дети
всей
земли*

СБОРНИК
ПЕСЕН

КИЙ ЯЗЫК»

SIEHE · HÖR ZU · LE

蛇 snake

3.6

蜜蜂

Set One

Japanese
Korean

Set Two

Cantonese
French

動物
拼圖識字卡

接龍遊戲　幼兒識字

貓
海
球
山
狗
鼠

bee

交
拼圖

We can see games in many languages.

動 物

拼 圖 識 字 卡

交

拼 圖

· SCHREIBE ·

接龍遊戲 幼兒識字

bee

3.18

butte

貓

海

球

山

狗

鼠

We can see games in many languages.

LA

There are over **6000** different languages spoken in the world today.

Abazinian ★ Abenaki ★ Agni ★ Ainu ★ Altai ★ Alu

Abkhazian ★ Afrikaans ★ Aleut ★ Algonkian ★ Aramaic ★ Assames

Akkadian ★ Albanian ★ Anyi ★ Apache ★ Arabic ★ Arunta ★ Azerbaijani ★ Banda

Ambo ★ Amharic ★ Araucanian ★ Avar ★ Arawak ★ Armenian ★ Aymara ★ Bambara ★ Bella

Arapaho ★ Assyrian ★ Athapascan ★ Avestan ★ Baluchi ★ Beaver ★ Beja ★ Blackfoot ★

Baining ★ Balante ★ Balinese ★ Balkar ★ Baule ★ Bislama ★ Burushaski ★ Cebuan

Bashkir ★ Basque ★ Batak ★ Bihari ★ Bikol ★ Burmese ★ Catalan ★ Chiga ★

Bengali ★ Berber ★ Bhili ★ Bhojpuri ★ Bulu ★ Carib ★ Carrier ★ Chickasaw ★ Choctaw ★

Bribri ★ Bubi ★ Buginese ★ Bulgarian ★ Cantonese ★ Cheyenne ★ Chiquito ★ Cornish ★ Cree

Cakchiquel ★ Cherokee ★ Chewa ★ Chippewa ★ Coptic ★ Chiquito ★ Cornish ★ Djerma ★

Cheremis ★ Chingpaw ★ Chipewyan ★ Comanche ★ Delaware ★ Dinka ★ Evenki ★

Chinese ★ Chungchia ★ Chuvash ★ Circassian ★ Dargin ★ Dari ★ Even ★ Frisia

Chungchia ★ Dakota ★ Danish ★ Esperanto ★ Estonian ★ French Creole ★ German ★ Gilal

Dagomba ★ Enga ★ English ★ Erse ★ Fon ★ Fox ★ French ★ Georgian ★ Gurma ★ Hmong ★ Ha

Enets ★ Finnish ★ Flathead ★ Flemish ★ Ge ★ Geez ★ Gujarati ★ Gurage ★ Interling

Galla ★ Ganda ★ Garo ★ Gbaya ★ Guaymi ★ Hindi ★ Hindustani ★ Ingush ★ Kalmyk ★ Kam

Greek ★ Greenlandic ★ Guarani ★ Hiligaynon ★ Ilocano ★ Indonesian ★ Kachin ★ Kazakh ★ Kekch

Hebrew ★ Hehe ★ Herero ★ Igorot ★ Ijaw ★ Kabre ★ Kabyle ★ Kawa ★ Kirgiz ★ Kissi ★ Kisw

★ Idoma ★ Kabardian ★ Kashubian ★ Kiowa ★ Kurukh ★ Kwakiutl ★ Lis

Jonkha ★ Kashmiri ★ Kingwana ★ Kurdish ★ Lilloeet ★ Lingala ★ Lwena ★ Malte

Karen ★ Kumyk ★ Lezgin ★ Luxembourgian ★ Malinke ★ Marshalle

bundu ★ ttish ★ divian ★ Min ★ Mina

How do we learn a language?

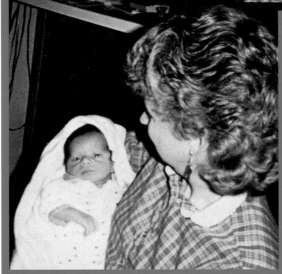

When we are very young,
we start listening and
learning the language
we hear spoken around us.

How do we become bilingual?

If we hear two languages, we can become bilingual. Some people learn to speak two, three, four, and more languages!

We can learn another language at any age. Sometimes we learn another language at school. Sometimes we learn another language when we visit or move to another country.

Paloma speaks two languages. She is bilingual in Spanish and English.

When Paloma was a baby, she heard her mother speak in Spanish, and her father speak in English.

Paloma's parents were waiting for the day when Paloma would say her first word. Would it be in English or in Spanish?

Would her first word be "mama" or "papa"? Paloma fooled everybody. Can you guess what her first word was?

It was "gato", which means "cat" in Spanish.

Paloma's Story

Paloma likes to read stories in Spanish to her mom and dad. Her father is learning Spanish, too.

Paloma also likes to make bilingual calendars in Spanish and English.

Paloma's mom works as a translator. She can translate English into Spanish, or Spanish into English.

A translator is a person who can read or hear what is being said in one language, and write or say it in another.

Once Paloma's mother went to Hawaii to work as a translator. Paloma got to go along. Paloma thinks being a translator would be fun.

Paloma's Story

Kai and Sau are bilingual in the Hmong and English languages. When they were very young, they heard their parents speak in Hmong. When they started school, they heard their teachers speak in English. Kai and Sau usually speak Hmong at home and English at school.

Sometimes the whole family goes to the farmer's market on weekends to sell arts and crafts made by the Hmong people.

After Kai and Sau help their mother set up the display, they sometimes go shopping for fresh fruits and vegetables at the market.

Kai and Sau's Story

Sau and Kai help their grandmother prepare the evening meal. They usually speak in Hmong to their grandmother, but sometimes their grandmother wants to learn some English words too. She is also becoming bilingual.

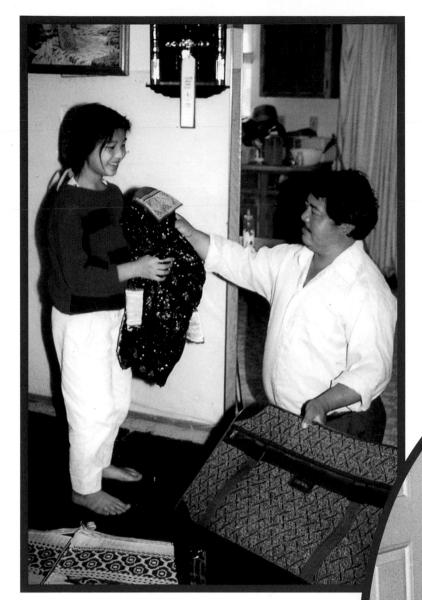

Once their father brought presents home for everybody. He brought a New Year's festival dress for Sau.

She will wear it when her family celebrates the New Year at a party with other Hmong families.

Kai and Sau's Story

Rosalie and Rosario live in the Philippine Islands. They are becoming bilingual in Tagalog and English.

At home, they usually speak in Tagalog with their family. At school, the teachers speak in Tagalog most of the day, but English is taught in one of the classes. Their teachers tell them that knowing more than one language will help them get good jobs when they grow up.

Rosalie and Rosario have special places to go in Manila, the city where they live. Their favorite place to have fun is at Luneta Park.

There they can climb giant stone dinosaurs and sea serpents. They can even tell secrets in the tail of a Stegasaurus!

Rosalie and Rosario's Story

One of their favorite places to shop is at the handicrafts market, where they can find things that are handmade by the Filipino people.

Once they bought a sungka game at the market. This game is played in many countries around the world and has many different names.

They also like to ride their bikes, and take boat rides around their city.

Rosalie and Rosario's Story

Every day, all around the world, we can
What language or languages do you spea

Abazinian ★ Abenaki ★ Abkhazian ★ Afrikaans ★ Agni ★ Ainu ★ Akkadian ★ A
Arabic ★ Aramaic ★ Aranda ★ Arapaho ★ Araucanian ★ Arawak ★ Armenian ★
Aymara ★ Azerbaijani ★ Babylonian ★ Bahnar ★ Baining ★ Balante ★ Baline
Basque ★ Bassa ★ Batak ★ Baule ★ Beaver ★ Beja ★ Bella Coola ★ Belorus
Blackfoot ★ Bodo ★ Brahui ★ Braille ★ Breton ★ Bribri ★ Bubi ★ Buginese ★ Bu
Cakchiquel ★ Cambodian ★ Cantonese ★ Carib ★ Carrier ★ Catalan ★ Cebua
Cheyenne ★ Chickasaw ★ Chiga ★ Chilcotin ★ Chimbu ★ Chin ★ Chinantec ★ (
Chol ★ Chontal ★ Chuang ★ Chukchi ★ Chungchia ★ Chuvash ★ Circassian ★ (
Dagbane ★ Dagomba ★ Dakota ★ Danish ★ Dargin ★ Dari ★ Delaware ★ Dink
Enga ★ English ★ Erse ★ Esperanto ★ Estonian ★ Even ★ Evenki ★ Ewe ★ Far
Fon ★ Fox ★ French ★ French Creole ★ Frisian ★ Friulian ★ Fukienese ★ Fular
Georgian ★ German ★ Gilaki ★ Gilbertese ★ Gilyak ★ Gisu ★ Gola ★ Gold ★ G
Gurma ★ Hadzapi ★ Hagen ★ Haida ★ Hakka ★ Harari ★ Hatsa ★ Hausa ★ Ha
Ho ★ Hopi ★ Hsiang ★ Huastec ★ Hungarian ★ Ibibio ★ Ibo ★ Icelandic ★ Inui
Iroquoian ★ Italian ★ Itelmen ★ Japanese ★ Jarai ★ Javanese ★ Jivaro ★ Jon
Kanarese ★ Kannada ★ Kanuri ★ Karachai ★ Kara-Kalpak ★ Karamojong ★ ★
Khakass ★ Khalkha ★ Khanty ★ Khasi ★ Kherwari ★ Khmer ★ Kiga ★ Kikuyu ★
Komi ★ Kongo ★ Konkani ★ Korean ★ Korku ★ Koryak ★ Kpelle ★ Krio ★ Kru ★
Lak ★ Lamut ★ Lango ★ Lao ★ Lappish ★ Latin ★ Latvian ★ Lenca ★ Lepcha ★ I
Lozi ★ Luba ★ Luganda ★ Lugbara ★ Lunda ★ Luo ★ Lusatian ★ Lushei ★ L
Magahi ★ Maithili ★ Makonde ★ Makua ★ Malagasy ★ Malay ★ Malayalam ★
Mangbetu ★ Mansi ★ Manx ★ Maori ★ Maranao ★ Marathi ★ Mari ★ Marind
Mazanderani ★ Mazatec ★ Mbum ★ Mbundu ★ Meithei ★ Mende ★ Micmac ★
Moldavian ★ Mon ★ Mongo ★ Mongolian ★ Mordvin ★ Moso ★ Mosquito ★ M
Nandi ★ Naskapi ★ Nauruan ★ Navajo ★ Ndebele ★ Nepali ★ Newari ★ Nez Pe
Nootka ★ Norwegian ★ Nubian ★ Nuer ★ Nung ★ Nupe ★ Nyamwezi ★ Nyanja ★
Oraon ★ Oriya ★ Osage ★ Ossetian ★ Ostyak ★ Otomi ★ Paiute ★ Palau ★ Pal
Passamaquoddy ★ Pawnee ★ Pedi ★ Pilipino ★ Pima ★ Pokot ★ Polish ★ Po
Rhade ★ Riffian ★ Romansch ★ Romany ★ Ruanda ★ Rumanian ★ Rundi ★ F
Santali ★ Sara ★ Saramacca ★ Sardinian ★ Savara ★ Sedang ★ Selkup ★ Sem
Shilluk ★ Shluh ★ Shona ★ Shoshone ★ Shuswap ★ Sibo ★ Sidamo ★ Sign ★ S
Sora ★ Sorbian ★ Sotho ★ Spanish ★ Suk ★ Sukuma ★ Sundanese ★ Susu ★ S
Taki-Taki ★ Tamashek ★ Tamazight ★ Tamil ★ Tarahumara ★ Tarasco ★ Tatar
Tibbu ★ Tibetan ★ Tigre ★ Tigrinya ★ Tiv ★ Tiwa ★ Tlingit ★ Tolai ★ Tonga ★ Tonga
Tuareg ★ Tulu ★ Tumbuka ★ Tung ★ Tungus ★ Tupi ★ Turkana ★ Turkish ★ Turkm
Urdu ★ Urhobo ★ Ute ★ Uvea ★ Uzbek ★ Vai ★ Venda ★ Vietnamese ★ Visa
Xhosa ★ Yabim ★ Yakima ★ Yakut ★ Yao ★ Yapese ★ Yi ★ Yiddish ★ Yoruba ★ S

see and hear many different languages.
? What languages would you like to learn?

anian ★ Aleut ★ Algonkian ★ Altai ★ Alur ★ Ambo ★ Amharic ★ Anyi ★ Apache
Arunta ★ Assamese ★ Assiniboin ★ Assyrian ★ Athapascan ★ Avar ★ Avestan
★ Balkar ★ Baluchi ★ Bambara ★ Banda ★ Bantu ★ Bari ★ Bariba ★ Bashkir
n ★ Bemba ★ Bengali ★ Berber ★ Bhili ★ Bhojpuri ★ Bihari ★ Bikol ★ Bislama
rian ★ Bulu ★ Burmese ★ Burushaski ★ Buryat ★ Bushman ★ Cabecar ★ Caddo
★ Chagga ★ Cham ★ Chamorro ★ Chechen ★ Cheremis ★ Cherokee ★ Chewa
nese ★ Chingpaw ★ Chipewyan ★ Chippewa ★ Chiquito ★ Choctaw ★ Chokwe
anche ★ Coptic ★ Cornish ★ Cree ★ Creek ★ Croatian ★ Crow ★ Cuna ★ Czech
★ Djerma ★ Duala ★ Dutch ★ Dyola ★ Dyula ★ Edo ★ Efik ★ Egyptian ★ Enets
alo ★ Fang ★ Fanti ★ Faroese ★ Farsi ★ Fijian ★ Finnish ★ Flathead ★ Flemish
★ Fur ★ Ga ★ Gaelic ★ Galician ★ Galla ★ Ganda ★ Garo ★ Gbaya ★ Ge ★ Geez
di ★ Grebo ★ Greek ★ Greenlandic ★ Guarani ★ Guaymi ★ Gujarati ★ Gurage
aiian ★ Hebrew ★ Hehe ★ Herero ★ Hiligaynon ★ Hindi ★ Hindustani ★ Hmong
★ Idoma ★ Igorot ★ Ijaw ★ Ilocano ★ Indonesian ★ Ingush ★ Interlingua ★ Irish
a ★ Kabardian ★ Kabre ★ Kabyle ★ Kachin ★ Kalmyk ★ Kamba ★ Kamchadal
aren ★ Kashmiri ★ Kashubian ★ Kawa ★ Kazakh ★ Kekchi ★ Keresan ★ Ket
mbundu ★ Kingwana ★ Kiowa ★ Kirgiz ★ Kissi ★ Kiswahili ★ Kituba ★ Klamath
ui ★ Kumyk ★ Kurdish ★ Kurukh ★ Kwakiutl ★ Ladin ★ Ladino ★ Lahnda ★ Lahu
ttish ★ Lezgin ★ Lillooet ★ Lingala ★ Lisu ★ Lithuanian ★ Lolo ★ Loma ★ Lotuko
vale ★ Luxembourgian ★ Lwena ★ Maba ★ Macedonian ★ Madi ★ Madurese
Maldivian ★ Malinke ★ Maltese ★ Mam ★ Manchu ★ Mandarin ★ Mandingo
Marquesan ★ Marshallese ★ Masai ★ Matabele ★ Maya ★ Mayo ★ Mazahua
Mien ★ Min ★ Minangkabau ★ Miskito ★ Mixe ★ Mixtec ★ Mohave ★ Mohawk
si ★ Motu ★ Mundari ★ Murmi ★ Murngin ★ Nahuatl ★ Nakhi ★ Nama ★ Nanai
ce ★ Nganasan ★ Nicobarese ★ Nimboran ★ Niuean ★ Nivkh ★ Nkole ★ Nogai
yankole ★ Nyoro ★ Occidental ★ Odul ★ Ojibwa ★ Okanagan ★ Omaha ★ Oneida
ng ★ Pampangan ★ Pangasinan ★ Panoan ★ Papago ★ Papiamento ★ Pashto
pean ★ Portuguese ★ Punjabi ★ Puyi ★ Quechua ★ Rajasthani ★ Rarotongan
ssian ★ Saho ★ Salar ★ Samaran ★ Samoan ★ Sandawe ★ Sango ★ Sanskrit
ole ★ Seneca ★ Senufo ★ Serbian ★ Serbo-Croatian ★ Serer ★ Shan ★ Shawia
dhi ★ Sinhalese ★ Sioux ★ Slovak ★ Slovenian ★ Somali ★ Songhai ★ Soninke
azi ★ Swedish ★ Syriac ★ Tabasaran ★ Tacana ★ Tadzhik ★ Tagalog ★ Tahitian
Tavgi ★ Teda ★ Telugu ★ Temne ★ Teso ★ Tewa ★ Thai ★ Thompson ★ Thonga
★ Toro ★ Totonac ★ Towa ★ Trukese ★ Tsimshian ★ Tsonga ★ Tswana ★ Tuamotu
n ★ Tuvinian ★ Twi ★ Tzeltal ★ Tzotzil ★ Udmurt ★ Uigur ★ Ukrainian ★ Umbundu
an ★ Vogul ★ Volapuk ★ Votyak ★ Wa ★ Welsh ★ Winnebago ★ Wolof ★ Wu
ucatec ★ Yukagir ★ Yuma ★ Yurak ★ Zande ★ Zapotec ★ Zoque ★ Zulu ★ Zuñi

About the Author

Claudia Schwalm has a BA from UC Berkeley and a Masters in Early Childhood Education. After ten years in the educational field, she left teaching in 1982 to found Claudia's Caravan, a children's multicultural book company. In 1998, she resumed her teaching career and now resides in Hayward, California. Her passions include photography, world travel, and helping children succeed. She has also written "Let's Count in Five Languages" and "Picture Dictionary in Six Languages".